Martin Luther

What should I do?

The true story of Martin Luther and the Reformation

Catherine Mackenzie
Illustrated by Rita Ammassari

Martin Luther was born in Germany in the year 1483. At fifteen years of age his parents sent him to a special school in Eisenach. This school had a strange custom. When Martin asked, 'What must I do to get my supper?' he was told, 'We have to sing for it!' So every night Martin and his friends would sing sweetly for anyone who would listen.

The boys loved it when they got something nice to eat before they went to bed.

Martin and his friends would sing sweetly for anyone who would listen.

Martin studied well and did what he was told. Teachers taught him his lessons in another language called Latin. The priests taught him about what the Pope and the Roman Catholic Church wanted him to do.

Unfortunately many of the things that the church taught at that time were not from the Bible.

Martin studied well and did what he was told.

Martin's parents wanted to make sure that their son became a rich man and was well respected. He was sent to university so that he would become a rich and important man. However, God and a thunderstorm put a stop to that.

Travelling on the road one day a streak of lightning came out of nowhere and almost struck Martin dead. Shaking with fear he promised that he would become a monk if only God would save his life. Martin felt that this was what he had to do.

A streak of lightning came
out of nowhere.

As a monk Martin often asked himself, 'What must I do to get God to forgive my sins?' Martin thought that he should pray for hours on end, eat very little, work very hard and study a great many good books. However, none of these things would ever get him to heaven. Instead of making things better, things only got worse.

Martin decided to visit the city of Rome where the Pope lived. The Pope was the head of the church. Surely in this amazing city Martin would find the answer he searched for. But he didn't.

Martin decided to visit the city of Rome.

On his return to Germany he was sent to Wittenberg to teach at the university there. A man called Johann von Staupitz encouraged him to read the Bible for himself.

When Martin opened the book of Romans he read the following words, 'He who through faith is righteous shall live.' Martin read more of God's Word and discovered that sinners could be saved and enter heaven – not by doing good things but by believing in the one true God.

Martin read more of God's Word.

Martin realised that he was not good enough to go to heaven. However, Jesus Christ was perfect and his death had purchased forgiveness of sins for all those who trusted in him. Being able to trust in God was something that Martin hadn't been able to do before – but now he could. God had given him the gift of faith.

Martin had been trying to save himself when the only person who could save him was God. From then on Martin taught the truth and not lies.

Martin realised that he was not good
enough to go to heaven.

One of the lies that people were told then was that they could buy a place in heaven. However, no amount of money could ever do that. Martin knew what he must do. On 31 October 1517, he wrote 95 theses (or concerns) about the teachings of the church. Martin nailed these sheets of paper to the door of the Castle Church in Wittenberg.

The Reformation had begun. Some people were very angry and even tried to arrest him so Martin had to flee for his life. However, a friend called Frederick the Wise, the ruler of Saxony protected him from his enemies.

Martin nailed these sheets of paper to the door.

Martin then had to appear before the Emperor, Charles V. This young man was very powerful and ruled over a large part of Europe. They met at a town called Worms and Martin was told that he must confess that he had spoken wrongly. Martin refused. He knew what he had to do.

'My conscience is captive to the word of God … It is neither safe nor right to go against conscience. Here I stand. I can do no other. May God help me. Amen.'

Martin then had to appear before the Emperor.

When he travelled home to Wittenberg something very frightening happened. Martin was kidnapped by a troop of horsemen and taken to a fortress near the town of Eisenach. To Martin's surprise, however, these horsemen were not his enemies. They had been sent by Frederick to rescue him from some men who were plotting to kill him.

Martin stayed in hiding for many months and during that time he translated the New Testament from Latin into German. This meant that ordinary German people could now read God's word for themselves.

Martin was kidnapped by a troop of horsemen.

Eventually Martin began to write books of his own. An amazing new invention called a printing press meant that it was very easy to make lots of books.

A woman called Katherine von Bora read Luther's books. She lived in a church building called a convent - a special building for women. If you lived there you were called a nun. But Katherine didn't want to be a nun anymore. So Katherine and her friends escaped by hiding in fish barrels in the back of a cart.

Katherine and her friends decided
to escape.

After spending some time in Wittenberg listening to Martin's preaching Katherine became Martin's wife. Martin called his wife Katie and they had a happy life together. But the Emperor was still very angry with Martin and the Reformers. However, many of the German princes agreed with Martin Luther's teachings.

The Reformation was growing. People today still read Martin's books. His teachings help many understand what the Bible really says and what God wants us to believe.

Martin called his wife Katie and they had a happy life together.

This book is written in memory of my grandparents:
William and Dolina Mackenzie and
Hugh and Catherine Mackay

**I will sing of the LORD's great love forever; with my mouth
I will make your faithfulness known through all generations.
Psalm 89:1**

© Copyright 2010 Catherine Mackenzie
ISBN: 978-1-84550-561-5
Published by Christian Focus Publications,
Geanies House, Fearn, Tain, Ross-shire, IV20 1TW,
Scotland, U.K.
www.christianfocus.com
Cover design by Daniel van Straaten
Printed in China
Other titles in this series:
Corrie ten Boom: Are all of the watches safe? 978-1-84550-109-9
Amy Carmichael: Can brown eyes be made blue? 978-1-84550-108-2
David Livingstone: Who is the bravest? 978-1-84550-384-0
John Calvin: What is the Truth? 978-1-84550-560-8
George Müller: Does money grow on trees? 978-1-84550-110-5
Helen Roseveare: What's in the parcel? 978-1-84550-383-3